THE SCHOOL OF SOLITUDE

THE SCHOOL OF SOLITUDE

LUIS HERNÁNDEZ

Translated and with a Foreword by Anthony L. Geist

Luis Hernández (Lima, 1941–Buenos Aires, 1977) was a Peruvian poet and physician who published three books by age 25, *Orilla, Charlie Melnick,* and *Las Constelaciones.* For the remainder of his short life he continued to write in notebooks, from which these poems are drawn.

Anthony Geist is professor of Spanish and Comparative Literature at the University of Washington. He is the author of numerous studies and translations of contemporary Spanish and Latin American poetry as well as a documentary film on the Lincoln Brigade, *Souls without Borders.*

Swan Isle Press, Chicago 60640-8790

Edition © 2015 by Swan Isle Press
© Los herederos de Luis Hernández
Translation © Anthony Geist

Swan Isle Press acknowledges with gratitude the support and encouragement of Max Hernández and Carlos Hernández, brothers of Luis Hernández, for their help in advancing the publication of this edition. Swan Isle Press also wishes to thank Pontificia Universidad Católica del Perú for providing from their digital archive facsimiles of Luis Hernández's notebooks which, along with Luis Hernández, *Vox Horrísona,* 3rd ed. Lima, Editorial Ave Fénix, provided the sources of poems and images for this edition.

19 18 17 16 15   12345
ISBN-13: 978-0-9833220-6-1 (paperback)

Swan Isle Press gratefully acknowledges the generous grant support from the University of Washington toward the publication of this bilingual edition of poetry.

Hernández, Luis, 1941-1977
    [Poems. Selections. English]
    The school of solitude: collected poems / Luis Hernández ; translated and with a foreword by Anthony L. Geist.
        pages cm
ISBN 978-0-9833220-6-1 (paperback)
1. Hernández, Luis, 1941-1977–Translations into English.   I. Geist, Anthony L., 1945- translator, writer of introduction.   II. Title.
    PQ8498.18.E67A2 2015
    861'.64–dc23

                        2015007946

This paper meets the requirements of ANSI/NISO Z39.48-1992 (Permanence of Paper).

Swan Isle Press gratefully acknowledges that this book has been made possible, in part, with the support of generous grants from:
University of Washington
Europe Bay Giving Trust

www.swanislepress.com

Contents

"The Blue Utterances of the Sun"

On Translating the Poetry of Luis Hernández

> "To know even hate
> Is but a mask of Love"
>
> ROBERT BROWNING

THERE IS A CERTAIN TRUTH to the adage that you don't truly understand a poem until you attempt to translate it. The exercise obliges you to account for each word, to seek equivalents in the target language for the complex syntactic structures peculiar to the source language, and to tread the fine line between the excessively literal and the excessively liberal. The irony, of course, and the beauty of translation is that the answers it offers open other sets of questions.

Luis (Lucho) Hernández (Lima, Peru, 1941—Santos Lugares, Argentina, 1977) is legendary in his native Peru, and virtually unknown outside it. His short, tragic life –haunted by addiction and periodic reclusion in rehabilitation centers—and the mysterious circumstances surrounding his death, have made him a cult figure. He is a poète maudit, in the tradition of Rimbaud and his countryman César Vallejo.

Hernández published three books of poetry: *Orilla* (1961), *Charlie Melnik* (1962), and *Las constelaciones* (1965). Though from age 24 until the end of his life, Hernández was not to publish again, he did not fall silent. He wrote in cheap, school-boy notebooks, filling them with poems, musical notations, quotes (attributed and unattributed), notes to himself, translations, musings, clippings from newspapers and comic strips, and drawings, all in different colored pencils and pens.

The notebooks appear to have been part of an ambitious project of "total poetry," yet Hernández apparently made no attempt to preserve or publish them. On the contrary, he gave them away to friends, family, other poets, even strangers he met in bars, and kept no record or copy of them. As a consequence, we probably will never know how many he produced or what has become of them. Today, those that we know are dispersed in private and public collections, mostly in Peru.

The poetry of the Hernández notebooks is born under the sign of Melancholy and Nostalgia. The poet evokes an irrevocably distant past from a desolate site in the present. Past happiness and joy, love and fulfillment, are remembered (remembered, re-assembled) in scraps and fragments, like shards of ancient pottery cast on a distant shore. Poetry can reconstruct but never recapture the past. Its totality always eludes us, lying just beyond our grasp. Melancholy resides precisely in the space between the capacity to recall and the impossibility of ever recovering the emotion and time once lived. The poet who records these memories is no longer the man who lived them. The poem serves to mark the unbreachable distance between then and now, the chasm between paradise lost and a season in hell.

Hernández evokes the memory of idyllic paradises –gardens, lakes, mountain villages, deserts, beaches—inhabited by the speaker and a "tú," variously identified as Apollo, Apollinian, or simply "you." Yet he recalls them (and himself) from present sites of decay, populated by barbed wire, leaky plumbing, rotting kelp, and departing ships that trail rust in their wake. The unresolved (and unresolvable) tension between then and now, presence and absence, plenitude and emptiness, joy and sorrow, is what gives these poems their emotional power. Hence the eight hauntingly beautiful elegies included here are as much a lament for the remembered self as for a lost past; they express sorrow more for the subject who was capable of feeling and losing happiness, than for the lost happiness itself.

Hernández is a postmodern plagiarist, as well. He borrows freely from other texts, cannibalizing and incorporating them into his own discourse, neither bothering to hide or acknowledge their traces. Thus the poem "Things Incompatible with Nietzsche" is a direct translation (perhaps Hernández's own) of a passage from *The Twilight of the Gods*. His only original contribution is the title and a typo he introduced into the Latin (*in impuribus naturalis* for *in impuribus naturalibus*). Yet one could argue that by presenting it as a poem and inscribing it in the larger context of the notebook, he makes Nietzsche's words his own.

Hernández's notebook poetry is full of obsessive repetitions and modulations of an image or a particular word or phrase. Often it is difficult to determine if certain texts are successive drafts of a single poem, or variations on a theme. Various alter egos and heteronyms surface and resurface sporadically in the notebooks. The poetic speaker assumes different personae: Billy the Kid, Luisito Hernández, a former boxing champion, Chief One-Side-of-the-Sky, Shelley Álvarez and others. What are we to make of this? Rather than the heroic Modernist subject, origin and generator of a coherent, unified discourse, we find a decentered subject who refers to himself alternately in first or third person. The shifting personal pronouns make it impossible to construct a stable identity for the speaker. Rather, a phantom subject flashes before us, a fragmented, postmodern subject, impossible to apprehend in any semblance of totality.

This same fragmentation, of course, is also articulated in the discourse of the notebook poetry, and this poses particular problems for the translator. The fluidity of his discourse makes meaning elusive and uncertain. His language is often unstable, signification slipping just beyond our reach, constantly sidestepping and shuffling, bobbing and weaving, like the welterweight he fancied himself to be.

One intuits emotion driving the words: sorrow, humor, loneliness, irony (though not ironic distance). But the emotion cannot drive language to completion. Instead, it breaks grammatical logic. Hernández's discourse is built on incomplete sentences, dangling clauses, half-finished thoughts and formulations:

If from the river should rise
Like rushes
Your life
And if mine

Or:

...And I shall no more
Die
And I shall no more.

Hernández camouflages his considerable erudition, burying references to the Old and New Testaments, classical music, and poetry written in various languages, under a psychedelic mixture of sex, drugs and rock 'n' roll, bottles of beer, Laurel and Hardy, pop culture, marihuana smoke and self-deprecation. The fact that this is visual poetry, in which Hernández fuses image and word through his calligraphy and drawing, complicates rather than illustrates meaning.

These are the challenges—and the rewards—that the Hernández notebooks hold for the translator and the reader. In trans-lating (that is, in moving the texts from one side to the other) I hope not to have fixed meaning in English but to have left the poems as open, ambiguous, and moving as they are in Spanish.

— ANTHONY L. GEIST
University of Washington

"Los cowboys
Cuando se gradúan
En la Escuela de la Soledad
En Melancolía
Escriben La Música
Que casi nunca
Ha Sido escuchada"

Poemas tristes
book the first

I

Los cowboys

Cuando se gradúan
En la Escuela de la Soledad

En Melancolía
Escriben la Música

Que casi nunca
Ha sido escuchada

Poemas tristes
book the first

Cowboys

When cowboys graduate
From the School of Solitude

With a degree in Melancholy
They write Music

That has almost never
Been heard

Sad Poems
book the first

El Sultán
tenía los
labios ámbar
por la pena
Junto al claro estanque
Un lúpulo verde
Que no olvido
Yo recuerdo
Aquél Tiempo
Con algo de Soledad
Alambres

II

[Soy Luisito Hernández]

Soy Luisito Hernández
Ex campeón
De peso welter
Y le dijeron:
Cuántas veces
Hemos de perdonar
Y él contestó
Setenta veces
Siete. Y como
Voy herido
Por la espalda
Sé hacia dónde
Voy. Y mi corazón
Sigue eligiéndote
Y un césped
Suave que crece
Al borde de la mar
Donde el Tiempo
Es fácil y vivir
Es de vidrio y
El les contestó
Setenta veces
Siete. Y sobre
Las colinas
Donde es tan claro
El tiempo

[This is Luisito Hernández]

This is Luisito Hernández
Former welterweight
Champion
And they asked him:
How many times
Must we forgive
And he replied
Seventy times
Seven. And because
I've been stabbed
In the back
I know where
I'm going. And my heart
Still chooses you
And soft
Grass growing
At the seashore
Where Time
Is easy and living
Is made of glass and
He answered them
Seventy times
Seven. And over
The hills
Where time
Is as clear

Y breve como
La Estación y
El contestó
Setenta veces
Siete. Hay sobre
El grass
El aire y las praderas
Contenido
Por las colinas silenciosas
Y él les contestó
Setenta veces
Siete

And short as
The Season and
He replied
Seventy times
Seven. Over
The hierba there is
Wind and prairies
Held
By the silent hills
And he answered them
Seventy times
Seven

[Y tú callabas]

Y tú callabas
Que es la vida
Callar
Ya lo sabías:
Si del río surgieran
Como juncos
Tu vida
Y si la mía

No recuerdo tus ojos
Pero sí lo que vieron

[And you fell silent]

And you fell silent
For life is
To be silent
As you well know:
If from the river should rise
Like rushes
Your life
And if mine

I don't remember your eyes
Only what they saw

La canción

M. Balakireff

Dicen que soy un soñador
Que sueña

Y otros dicen de mí

Adiós. Me voy a otro lugar
Y si la tristeza
Me alcanza
Y si la tristeza me alcanza
Me cubriré con el agua
De la mar. Y no he más
De morir
Y no he más.

The Song

M. Balakireff

They say I am a dreamer
Who dreams

And others say of me

So long. I'm going to another place
And if sorrow
Catches up with me
And if sorrow catches up with me
I'll bury myself in the depths
Of the sea. And I shall no more
Die
And I shall no more.

Alambres

Como se adormece
El tiempo y el pasar
Del agua yo
Me recuerdo aún
Cuando el sol
Era en tus ojos

Y la música
Subía como
La niebla sobre
Las praderas

O la extensa playa

Tú oías la canción

Wires

Just as time
And the passage of water
Drifts into sleep I
Still recall myself
When the sun
Rose in your eyes

And music
Settled like
Fog on
The plains

Or the expanse of beach

You heard the song

Apollon Musagète

Apolo coronado
Por Laureles
Y Hardys

Hay una calma
Que es la paz
De las seis

Al salir
Del cinema

Y es la calma
Diaria que lleva

La Mar aun
En el golpe de luz

De la tormenta
Y la costa
Al pie de los acantilados
La tierra agrietada
De los
Acantilados

Para ver el mar

Apollon Musagète

Apollo crowned
With Laurels
And Hardys

There is a calm
That's the peace
You feel

At six o'clock as
You leave the movie house

And it's the everyday
Calm borne on

The Sea even
In the bolt of light

From a storm
And the coast
At the foot of cliffs
The cracked earth
Of the
Cliffs

Desde lo alto

Y el aire de la mar

Apolo quebrado
Por telarañas

Heliconio

To catch sight of the sea
From on high

And the sea breeze

Apollo shattered
On cobwebs

Heliconian

[Los laureles]

Los laureles
Se emplean
En los poetas
Y en los tallarines

[Laurel Leaves]

Laurel leaves
Crown
Both poets
And pasta

Prélude

a FEDERICO CHOPIN

¿Recuerdas tú
El bosque de Watteau

Y un claro de luna
Que sí ha de volver
Que sí volverá?

¿Recuerdas tú?

2

Y si recuerdas
El bosque

Dónde habré
De hallarte

Recordando

Prélude

1

to FRÉDÉRIC CHOPIN

Do you remember
Watteau's woods

And a claire de lune
That must return
That shall return?

Do you remember?

2

And if you remember
The woods

Where shall I
Find you

Remembering

[El sultán tenía...]

El sultán tenía
Los labios ámbar
Por la pena
Junto al claro
Estanque
Un verde lúpulo
Que no olvido
Yo recuerdo aquel
Tiempo
Con algo
De soledad

Alambres

[The Sultan's lips...]

The Sultan's lips
Turned amber
With sorrow
At the edge
Of the clear pond
A green hops vine
That I'll never forget
I remember that
Time
With a twinge
Of loneliness

Barbed wire

El origen de Darwin según el mono

Darwin nació frente a las turbulencias del Atlántico, uno de los lagos mayores de los humanos. Tendenciosamente, luego, no proclamó (porque era un sabio) sino insinuó que la mente del hombre tiene derecho a habitar en cualquiera de los mundos de la creación.

Sobre el mar, llevado en un navío, sobre el mar escarlata, llegó al Archipiélago múltiple de las Islas Galápagos.

Ahí vio los misterios de la simpleza, los misterios de la vida, el estaño, los dátiles, el helio.

Como ven, fue un gran náufrago. Arriba tengo su libro.

The Origin of Darwin
according to the Apes

Darwin was born on the shores of the turbulent Atlantic, one of the largest lakes known to man. Contentiously, then, he did not proclaim (for he was a wise man) but insinuated that the human mind has the right to inhabit any of the worlds of creation.

Over the sea, transported in a ship, over the scarlet sea, he arrived at the multiple Archipielago of the Galapagos.

There he saw the mysteries of simplicity, the mysteries of life, tin, date palms, helium.

As you can see, he was a great man marooned. I've got his book upstairs.

Homenaje a Shakespeare

La Poesía
Es un Arte
Bill

Homage to Shakespeare

Poetry
Is a Billain's
Art

III

[Cuando quiero escribir]

Cuando quiero escribir
Algo no lo hago

Porque la serenidad
Y la tristeza

La risa
O el teléfono

Me pretextan

Hacia la vagancia

[When I want to write]

When I want to write
Something I don't

Because serenity
And sorrow

Laughter
Or the telephone

Alibi me

Toward indolence

[No he de volver a escribir]

No he de volver a escribir
Como lo hice
Cuando el corazón era joven
Y sobre mí el firmamento

Ahora no te pido, Señor,
El olvido, sino
Lo que no conocí

[I shall never write again]

I shall never write again as
I did when hearts were young
And, shimmering above me,
The firmament

I do not ask thee, Lord,
For oblivion, but for all
I never knew

[Si cantara]

Si cantara
Lo que en el corazón
Siento

Sería para mí

La canción

Algo indescifrable

[If I were to sing]

If I were to sing
What in my heart
I feel

It would be for me

An indecipherable

Song

El poema

Los ojos del niño Mozart
Son los ojos de los niños
De esta Tierra. Los ojos

Del torturado cuerpo
Del poeta Arturo Rimbaud
Son los ojos de todos
Los niños del mundo. Las jerarquías

De los Angeles son: Angeles,
Arcángeles, Tronos,
Potestades, Dominaciones,
Querubines y Serafines.

The Poem

The child Mozart's eyes
Are the eyes of all the children
On this Earth. The eyes

Of the tortured body
Of the poet Arthur Rimbaud
Are the eyes of all
The children in the world. The hierarchies

Of the Angels are: Angels,
Archangels, Thrones,
Powers, Dominions,
Cherubim and Seraphim.

At Dusk

Atardezco
Navego por los ríos

Cuya luz

Es grata hacia mis ojos
Y se esconde
Lentamente
Entre la noche.

At Dusk

Night falls within me
I sail down rivers

Whose light

Caresses my eyes
And fades
Slowly
Into the night.

[Nunca he sido feliz]

Nunca he sido feliz
Pero, al menos,
He perdido
Varias veces
La felicidad.

[I have never been happy]

I have never been happy
But, at least,
A number of times
I have lost
Happiness.

A Luis Cernuda

Es el Sur
Quien nos lleva
Y nos olvida

Hacia el alba postrera

Sus presagios

Aprendidos sin miedo
En las estrellas

Son tan sólo la forma
Como el agua

Ha llegado
Centellante

To Luis Cernuda

It is the South
That transports us
And foresakes us

Toward the final break of dawn

Its omens

Fearlessly studied
In the stars

Are mere form
Like water

Shimmering
It has arrived

A Rainer María Rilke
Val Mont 1926
o
El Espectro de la Rosa

Silencioso amigo de las muchas lejanías

Mi ilusión única
Es el verte

Verte es una de tanta
Ilusión

Tu rostro ennoblece
La plenitud de la noche
Pues Amor
Jamás abandonó
Tus ojos: leve, tenue

Y alguien
Te hablará
De mí, de tanta
Ilusión:
La menos ilusa
La más real

To Rainer María Rilke
Val Mont 1926
or
The Specter of the Rose

Silencioso amigo de las muchas lejanías

My only hope
Is seeing you

Seeing you is one full of
Hope

Your face makes noble
The fullness of night
For Love
Has never left
Your eyes: weightless, faint

And someone
Shall speak to you
Of me, of so much
Hope:
The most hopeful
The least unreal

Es verte
Había un jardín

Cómo lo he de olvidar.

Is seeing you
There was a garden

How can I forget.

Bach es capito

Bach es capito
El Concierto Brandenburgués
Número cinco
Es la cumbre
Del ciclismo.
Entre la cumbre
Y la profundidad
Median las almas

Bach is Boss

Bach is Boss
The Brandenburg Concerto
Number five
Is the peak
Of bike racing.
Between the peak
And the depths
Range the souls

El tercer planeta

velut prati

A 150 millones de kilómetros del sol, cubierta del mar Indico y otras extensiones del océano se oye el sonido del tercer planeta: gaseosas, maderas, música para violín, 'cello y piano. Desde la tierra el sol se ve como un disco naranja Fanta, como tablones o un helado cometa en la Estepa del cielo (bene, bien, well). Este es el tercer planeta; el primero es Mercurio, que también se usa en los termómetros; el segundo Venus, la pluvial, y, el tercero, la tierra, único planeta del sistema solar donde se permite lo que se permite. La situación política es sencilla: los pueblos se dividen en: pueblos que se alimentan y pueblos gobernados por generales. Estos últimos proceden de escuelas donde se grita, se hace movimientos en serie y se sale los sábados. La niebla cubre la mañana del domingo con una impalpable música. Y el corazón crece.

Fin del documental sobre el Tercer Planeta.

The Third Planet

velut prati

150 million kilometers from the sun, covered by the Indian Ocean and other expanses of the ocean is heard the sound of the third planet: soda pop, lumber, music for violin, cello and piano. From the earth the sun looks like an Orange Crush sign, like boards or a frozen kite in the heavenly steppes (bene, bien, well). This is the third planet; the first is Mercury, which is also used in thermometers; the second, Venus, the rainy, and the third, Earth, the only planet in the solar system where what is allowed is allowed. The political situation is quite simple: the people are divided into: people who have enough to eat, and people who are ruled by generals. The latter come from schools where they shout, where they move in unison, and where they go out on Saturday. Fog covers Sunday morning with an intangible music. And the heart swells.

End of documentary on the Third Planet.

and the tongue of
the dumb shall sing

Viento del Oeste
De dónde vienes
Dile a aquél que escribió
Su nombre
Entre las aguas

IV

Elegía primera

Close bosom friend of the maturing sun
Conspiring with him how to load and bless
With fruit the vines...

KEATS

Llevaría entonces
Hacia ti tu jardín

Que es el mar
Donde ha tiempo
Que ensueñas

El reposo
Y las frases
Azules del Sol

Y así tal vez
Te dijera

Cómo te amo

Y en la orilla
Distante la bruma
Nos contemplaba:

Elegy Number One

Close bosom friend of the maturing sun
Conspiring with him how to load and bless
With fruit the vines...

KEATS

Your garden surely
Led to you then

Your garden that is the sea
Where for years
You have dreamt

Repose
And the blue
Utterances of the Sun

And so perhaps
I told you

The ways of my love

And on the distant
Shore the mist
Gazed upon us:

Era la tarde
Y tú sin prisa

Tú jugabas con los sortilegios
Del agua en la juntura

Gastada y con las algas
Del silente muelle

Oh, llévame contigo,
Yo que reconozco

Tu sonreír
Y tus ojos

Y con las algas

It was evening
And you, unhurried,

You toyed with omens
Cast by water in the worn

Plumbing and with kelp
On the silent pier

Oh, take me with you,
I who recall

Your way of smiling
And your eyes

And with the kelp

Elegía segunda

Y azul el Tiempo

Se extiende
Sobre el páramo

Exótico:
                    Así también

(Tan continuo
Es el cielo

Como aquellas
Dunas. Como

El Desierto
Esbelto e inolvidable)

Perdona: pero
Yo no sé de otro

Mar más lejano
Ni otra noche

Más lenta
Pero conozco

Elegy Number Two

And Time tumbles

Blue
Over the exotic

Wasteland:
                    So too

(The sky is
As endless

As those
Dunes. As

The sleek, unforgettable
Desert)

Forgive me: but
I know no other

Sea more distant
Nor another night

More slow
But I do know

Del instante
En que ha de surgir

La dicha

(No como algo
Tenue o moderato,

Sino como
Una estrella

Donde sumergir
El rostro

Una estrella
Donde beber

De la luz)

Centellante

Ahí es que oirás
De la brisa:

Los pétalos gigantescos
Del Estío.

Hasta que la noche
Advenga.

The moment
When joy

Will arise

(Not as something
Tenuous or moderato

But like
A star

To plunge
Your face in

A star
Where you can drink

Deeply of light)

Shimmering

That is where you will
Hear from the wind:

The giant petals
Of Summer.

Until night
Falls.

Tercera elegía

La fiebre de una hermosa caravana triunfal
ABRAHAM VALDELOMAR

una a una las olas
gastaron nuestras vidas
PABLO NERUDA

…pero sé
Del instante

En que ha
De surgir la dicha

Como el mar
Que dejaste

Por contemplar
La playa

No conozco
De ti sino la sombra

Conque besas
Al Tiempo

Elegy Number Three

La fiebre de una hermosa caravana triunfal
ABRAHAM VALDELOMAR

una a una las olas
gastaron nuestras vidas
PABLO NERUDA

…but I do know
The moment

When joy will
Arise

Like the sea
You turned from

To gaze on
The shore

I know nothing
But your shadow

That kisses
Time

No conozco
De ti sino la flor
Alada

El extraño
Fulgor

                 (hay en ciertas
almas

como una cualidad
inexplicable)

Que percibo
En las cosas

Si te acercas

Pero de tus labios
O tu cuerpo

No conozco
Sino el estruendo

De los árboles
Y el sol

I know nothing
Of you but the winged
Blossom

The strange
Glow

                 (in certain souls
there's such

a mysterious
quality)

That I perceive
In things

If you draw near

Though of your lips
Or your flesh

I know nothing
But thunder

In the trees
And the Sun

Cuando tus manos
O tu sombra

En esta calle

When your hands
Or your shadow

Down this street

Cuarta elegía

El extraño fulgor
Que percibo en las cosas

Si te acercas:

El color
Que hay en tus ojos
Tras el bosque
¿Podrá ser
El exacto color
Que yo silente
Observo?: pues también
De Amor. El color

Elegy Number Four

deja que el sol se lleve
las tardes que nos quedan en la vida
ABRAHAM VALDELOMAR

una a una las olas
gastaron
nuestras vidas
PABLO NERUDA

Hope, love, doubt, desire,
Which consume him forever
SHELLEY

The strange glow
That I perceive in things

If you draw near:

The color
That glints in your eyes
Through the trees
Can it be
The exact color
I silently
Observe?: of Love
As well. The color

De la playa que dejamos
Ardiendo en la luz
Que precede
A los muelles

Y elevada
En los muros

Llama en tu ayuda
Al Tiempo

Llama a las flores:

Y tú, a merced
De los melancólicos

Muros de la mar

Sigues entonando
De la arena

La canción amada
Esta tarde

Tal vez de gaviotas
De geranios

Of the shore we left
Burning in the light
That comes before
The docks

And high
Upon the walls

Calls Time
To your side

Calls the flowers:

And you, at the mercy
Of the melancholy

Walls of the sea

Chant over and over
The sands'

Beloved song
This afternoon

Gulls' song perhaps
Geraniums'

Sólo la emoción
Perdura.

Only emotion
Endures.

Quinta elegía

Yo solo cruzo su silencio

ABRAHAM VALDELOMAR

Hoy das
Al mar
De Agua Dulce
El único relato

Solamente
Que ahora
Es tu cuerpo vencido

Un tiempo
Un tiempo de
Amor. Tan
Silencioso soy

Que tu recuerdo
Me permite la dicha

Y el óxido tenue
Que dejan
Las embarcaciones
Tras partir. Tan
Silencioso soy
Que si yo

Elegy Number Five

Yo solo cruzo su silencio

ABRAHAM VALDELOMAR

Today you bestow on
On the sea
Of Agua Dulce Beach
Its only story

It's just that
Now
Your spent body is

A time
A time of
Love. So
Silent am I

That your memory
Grants me joy

And the faint trace
Of rust that ships
Trail in their wake
As they depart. So
Silent am I
That were I

Cantase brotarían
A la vez

De las claras
Vertientes, a la vez
De la luz

Y la espuma
Llameante

Enredaderas
Tan silencioso soy
Que tu recuerdo

Me permite la dicha

To sing
At the same time

From the clear
Slopes, at the same time
From the light

And flickering foam
Would spring forth

Twining tendrils
So silent am I
That your memory

Grants me joy

Sexta elegía

yo -dice él- estoy
un poco echado
a perder.

Y no hay melancolía
en sus palabras;
hay una indiferencia,
una resignación,
un abandono

AZORÍN

Hoy das al Mar
De Agua Dulce
El único relato

Tan sólo que la playa

Es para ti un tiempo
Un tiempo de amor:

Tan silencioso soy
Que tu recuerdo
Me permite la dicha

Y el óxido tenue

Elegy Number Six

yo –dice él—estoy
un poco echado
a perder.

Y no hay melancolía
en sus palabras;
hay una indiferencia,
una resignación,
un abandono

AZORÍN

Today you bestow on
The Sea of Agua Dulce Beach
Its only story

Just that the beach

Is for you a time
A time of love:

So silent am I
That your memory
Grants me joy

And the faint trace of rust

Que dejan

Algunas embarcaciones
Tras partir

Tan silencioso soy
Que de hablar

Brotarían a la vez
De la luz
A la vez de las claras
Vertientes, el musgo,
Las algas

Y una clara sensación
De haberte visto

Tan silencioso soy
Que tu recuerdo
Me permite la dicha

That some ships

Trail in their wake
As they depart

So silent am I
That were I to speak

At the same time
From the light
At the same time from the clear
Slopes, would spring forth
Moss, kelp

And a clear sense
Of having seen you

So silent am I
That your memory
Grants me joy

Séptima elegía

Elegía en Garmisch
Parten - Kirchen
a RICHARD STRAUSS

Y, a lo lejos.
Los Alpes,

Los amados
De la nieve
Y de la sombra

                                   añil

Donde se quiebra
El agua
Para que de ella
Brote el Arbol
De la Música
Cuyo inolvidable
Fruto y la nieve
Y la gigantesca
Sombra
De la Melancolía
Im Abendrot. Así
Hemos llegado
A través
Del bosque deleitoso

Elegy Number Seven

Elegía en Garmisch
Parten – Kirchen
to RICHARD STRAUSS

And, in the distance,
The Alps,

The beloved of
Snow
And indigo

          shadows
Where waters
Part
For the Tree
Of Music
To burst forth
Whose unforgettable
Fruit and the snow
And the immense
Shadow
Of Melancholy
Im Abendrot. Thus
We have emerged
From
The woods of delight

Donde habitan
La Armonía
Y el cantar:
Ahí has de ver
La flor
Que en el brocal
Se anuda al agua:
Aquel agua
Donde reside
El Sol

Where harmony
And song
Dwell:
There you shall see
The flower
That on the berm
Entwines with the water:
That very water
Where the Sun
Resides

Octava elegía

Creo que lo mejor
Que me sucedió
Fue el haberte
Conocido

Creo que no hubo
Algo mejor el agua

Del Mar Austral:

Tú rasgabas
La arena
Como una pradera
Suave
Por la que no debe

Elegy Number Eight

de un gualdo intenso,
con intensas flores bermejas,
con intensos ramajes verdes.

AZORÍN

im Abendrot
in the yellow leaf
porque para vivir sólo hay que ser
o un animal o un Dios
ARISTÓTELES

I think the best thing
That ever happened to me
Was meeting
You

I think there was
Nothing better the waters

Of the Southern Seas:

You traced lines in
The sand
Like a gentle
Prairie
Where doubts

Ya jamás el preguntarse
Creo que lo mejor

¿How can I tell
You about my love?

Fue haberte conocido

Creo que es lo único
Que me sucedió

Must never
I think the best thing

¿Cómo puedo hablarte
De mi amor?

Was meeting you

I think it was the only thing
That ever happened to me

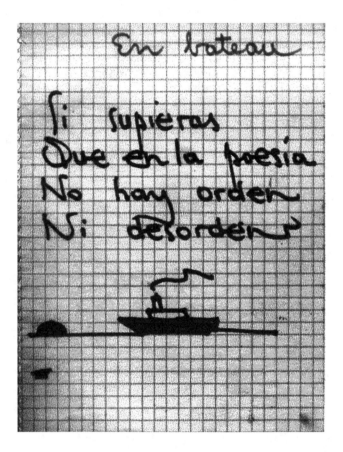

v

[Una forma...]

Una forma
De escribir poesía
Es vivir epigrafiando

[One way...]

One way
Of writing poetry
Is to live epigraphically

Cosas incompatibles
con Nietzsche

Séneca, o el torero de la virtud.

Rousseau o el retorno a la Naturaleza,
    in impuribus naturalis.

Schiller: el trompetista moral de Sackingen.

Dante: la hiena que escribe poemas
    entre las tumbas.

Kant: el "cant" como carácter inteligible.

Víctor Hugo: el faro en el mar del absurdo.

Liszt: la escuela de la velocidad, para correr
    tras las mujeres.

George Sand: láctea ubertas, la vaca de leche
    con un "bello estilo".

Michelet: el pesimismo como comida que se repite.

Stuart-Mill: la claridad que ofende.

Things Incompatible
with Nietzsche

Seneca, or the matador of virtue.

Rousseau or the return to Nature
in *impuribus naturalis.*

Schiller: the moral trumpeter of Sackingen.

Dante: the hyena who writes poems
in the graveyard.

Kant: "cant" as intelligible character.

Victor Hugo: lighthouse in the sea of absurdity.

Liszt: school of speed, to chase
chicks.

George Sand: láctea ubertas, the dairy cow
with a "beautiful style."

Michelet: pessimism as a meal that repeats on you.

Stuart-Mill: offensive clarity.

Les fréres Goncourt: dos Ayax frente a Homero.

Música de Offenbach.

Zola: el placer de oler mal.

The brothers Goncourt: two Ajaxes facing Homer.

Music by Offenbach.

Zola: the pleasure of stinking.

[Invierte...]

Invierte en peligro
Y ganarás
En seguridad

[Invest...]

Invest in danger
And you will gain
In security

Self-portrait

Soy Billy th' Kid
Ladrón de bancos
Y como llevo una herida
En la espalda y como
El tiempo muchas veces
Me negó sus aguas

Sé dónde voy:

Gracias Desierto
Y nunca olvidaré
Tus pasos sobre
La arena. Tú jamás
Olvidarás los míos.

Y bajo el sol del Poniente
Im Abendrot.

La línea misma
Del crepúsculo
Es la línea de la Aurora

Soy Luis Hernández
Y sé dónde voy

Self-Portrait

I'm Billy th' Kid
Bank-robber
And since I have a bullet
In my back and since
Time has often
Denied me its waters

I know where I'm going:

Thank you Desert
And I'll never forget
Your tracks in
The Sand. You'll never
Forget mine.

And under the Western sun
Im Abendrot.

The very line
Of Dusk
Is the line of Dawn

I'm Luis Hernández
And I know where I'm going

Esto va diziendo
E las yentes se allegando

Y sé dónde he de ir

Y el no soñar
Se asemeja al ensueño

Pero La Poesía
No es la Demencia

Es más bien aquello
Con tu añil claridad
Porque el tiempo es breve
Según al igual el Verano

An unusual Beauty

Passando van las sierras
e los montes e las aguas

Y ante mí se extiende
El Desierto vacuo

Y transparente
Y no pervive

Sólo La Emoción perdura
Sólo La Armonía quiebra

Esto va diziendo
E las yentes se allegando

And I know where I must go

And not dreaming
Resembles day-dreaming

But Poetry
Is not Dementia

It is more like something
With your indigo clarity
For time is fleeting
As too is Summer

An unusual Beauty

Passando van las sierras
E los montes e las aguas

And before me stretches
The transparent vacant

Desert
And it does not prevail

Only Emotion endures
Only Harmony shatters

El esplendente silencio

De la noche y alguien

Le dijo: Maestro,
Cuántas veces debemos
Perdonar. Y él les
Respondió setenta
Veces siete

*Alegres están todas
las yentes*

The splendent silence

Of night and someone

Said: Master,
How many times must we
Forgive. And he
Told them seventy
Times seven

Alegres están todas
las yentes

[Llevo mi corazón]

Llevo mi corazón
cubierto
por un mar
desconocido:
Por una mar
arcana
y te entristecerás
de mí

Solo la emoción
Perdura

No así el verso

[My heart lies]

My heart lies
awash
in an unknown
sea:
In an arcane
sea
and you will feel sorrow
for me

Only emotion
Endures

Not so poetry

[Yo hubiera sido]

Yo hubiera sido
Premio Nobel
De Física

Pero el mar
La cerveza

Y un amor

Me lo impidieron

[I would have been]

I would have been
A Nobel Prize
In Physics

But the sea
A can of beer

And a lover

Got in the way

En bateau

Si supieras
Que en la poesía
No hay orden
Ni desorden

En bateau

If you only knew
That in poetry
There is neither order
Nor disorder

Qué laberinto

Qué laberinto
Y qué amor
Es la poesía

Such a maze

Such a maze
And such love
Is poetry

El Estanque Moteado

Conocí a un Empirista inglés (era yo). El Empirismo inglés consistía en ver las cosas tal cual son, pasear por la playa y beber cerveza. Cerveza nocturna de los parques: paz de los bares, paz de los cinemas, donde el Tiempo es fácil y estalla como los prismas diminutos en la arena de plexiglass. Y un amor:

1   La Sensación

Los sentidos son muchos pero se reducen, retroceden y tiemblan ante la emoción. Esto no significa que nuestra percepción esté contaminada por la emoción, sino, más bien, emocionada. Si yo coloco un sol en la Wurlitzer de un bar donde no bebería dada mi condición social, oiré *Un gato en la oscuridad*.

2   Adelante, mortales, a llenar los corazones de sueños

Para comprender la vida es indispensable no aterrarse ante el laberinto intrincado de árboles, sol y aire que rodean la noche. Nada hay en el intelecto que no haya pasado antes por el intelecto, musitó Leibnitz mientras jugaba a nadar con el alma. Cuando amanece la playa se puebla de bañistas, triciclos, helados, y el ensueño de las grandes urbes.

The Mottled Pond

I once knew an English Empiricist (it was me). English Empiricism consists of seeing things as they are, walking on the beach and drinking beer. Nocturnal beer in parks: peace of taverns, peace of movie theaters, where Time is easy and explodes like tiny prisms in plexiglass sand. And a love:

1   Sensation

The senses are numerous but they shrink, retreat and tremble in the face of emotion. This does not mean that our perception is polluted by emotion, but rather, that it is moved. If I drop a quarter in the jukebox in a bar where, given my social status, I normally would not drink, I will hear *A Cat in the Dark*.

2   Onward, mortals, fill your hearts with dreams

To understand life it is absolutely necessary not to be terrified by the intricate maze of trees, sun and wind that surround night. There is nothing in our intellect that has not come from our intellect, pondered Leibnitz, as he played at swimming with his soul. At daybreak the beach fills with bathers, tricycles, ice cream cones, and the daydreams of great cities.

El libro de los Desiertos

Chanson
1

Anciano Desierto
Tú también cantas

Tu canción
De duna y sal

2

O aquellos Desiertos,
Ausente la mar
Ante la mirada
De la arena

Y tú llegabas
A través de las dunas,
Ruinas de tristezas:

Aquello es demasiado
Dorado: no digas
Nada del sol:

La misma soledad

Book of the Deserts

Chanson

I

Ancient Desert
You too sing

Your song
Of dunes and salt

2

Or those Deserts
Absent the sea
Under the gaze
Of the sand

And you arrived
Over the dunes,
Ruins of sorrow:

That is too
Golden: say
Nothing of the sun:

The very solitude

Del Desierto
Lo salvará
De ser un solitario

finale

3

Allí el mar
Y más cerca aún
La noche:

Esta es la soñada
Coherencia

Of the desert
Will save him
From being solitary

finale

3

Over there the sea
And nearer still
The night:

This is the coherence
We have dreamt of

*

Los laureles
se emplean
En los poetas
Y en los tallarines

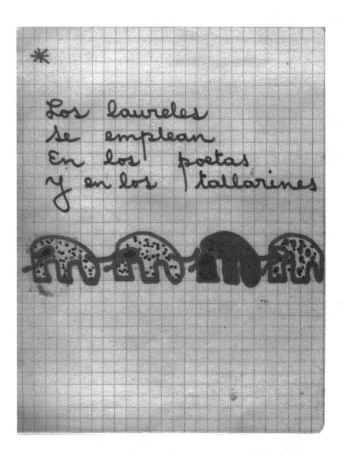

VI

Apolo azul

Te asemejas a algunos poetas,
Siempre cercano al cielo,
O, si se quiere, a los techos,
Como Claudel. Y algo ligeramente cabro
Como Rimbaud. Apolíneo algunas veces
Y otras simplemente en onda;
Cuando danzas seguido por las musas
Esas nueve pamperas
De las cuales mi favorita
Es la de la Astronomía.

Te pareces a algunos músicos.
A Strawinsky, por ejemplo,
Que compite en belleza contigo
Y es un poco más inmortal,
O a Carlos Ives, quien te gana
En misterio.

Tienes un aire a algunos gimnastas,
A ciertos dioses,
A ningún político,
A ningún papa.

En una palabra:
Eres Apolo
Y eso nadie te lo quita.

Blue Apollo

You resemble certain poets,
Always close to heaven,
Or, if you prefer, near the ceiling,
Like Claudel. And slightly queer
Like Rimbaud. Apollinean at times
And at others simply hip;
When you dance followed by the Muses
Those nine sluts
Of which my favorite
Is the muse of Astronomy.

You are like certain composers.
Stravinsky, for instance,
Your equal in beauty
And a bit more immortal,
Or Charles Ives, who wins hands down
In mystery.

You have an air of certain gymnasts,
Certain gods,
Not politicians,
Much less Popes.

In a word:
You are Apollo
And there's no getting around it.

Chanson d'amour: Tu corazón

Tu corazón
Se parece
Como una gota de agua
A otro corazón

Chanson d'amour: Your heart

Your heart
Is like
One pea in a pod
With another heart

Poemas tristes

1 Chanson d'amour

Perdóname el no haber
Muerto de Amor
Por ti. Es imperdonable.

Perdóname que mi Amor
No te ayude.

Perdóname que mi amor
No te importe

2

Sin ti, es inexplicable
Beber la Coca Cola
Helada da lo mismo
Que patear una lata

3

Estoy triste
Porque no estás;
Y no lloraré

Poems of Sorrow

1 Chanson d'amour

Forgive me for not
Dying of Love
For you. It's inexcusable.

Forgive my Love
For not helping you.

Forgive my love
For not mattering to you

2

Without you, it's inexplicable
Drinking ice cold
Coke is the same
As kicking a can

3

I'm sad
Because you're gone;
And I won't cry

Porque luego
Los ojos
No son lo mismo.

Because then
My eyes
Won't be the same.

Serenata amorosa

tú me quemabas, Atis
con tu boca pequeña
FRANÇOIS MAURIAC

Nada sé de ti
Sino la forma
Como el sol muriente
Recibe tu figura

Yo no conozco de ti
El día, el cierzo,
La sucesión del mar
Cantando tu huida

La palabra bella,
El Ambar. No los sé:
Sólo presiento
Tu rostro

Sólo sospecho
Tu voz

Sólo el dolor
Si es que ausente

Dime si es la luz

Love Serenade

You scorched me, Atis,
with your fine mouth.

FRANÇOIS MAURIAC

I know nothing of you
But the way
The dying sun
Welcomes your body

I know nothing of you
The day, the south wind,
Singing, wave after wave
Your retreat.

The perfect word,
Ambar. I know them not:
I can only sense
Your face

I can only imagine
Your voice

Only sorrow
In absence

Tell me if it's the light

Aquello que se anuda

A tu sombra o tal vez
La huella
Que en tus manos:
La huella
de
la
luna

That's tangled

Around your shadow or perhaps
The trace
That in your hands:
The trace
of
the
moon

A Federico Hölderlin

Tan lejos de ti mismo
Como cerca
Del duro y sacro reino
En espera del sol
Junto al cielo naranja

Tan cerca

En espera del sol
Tras una tapia
De maderas
Hierba en el suelo

Y titubeas ante todo
Ante el cielo
Ante los dos rostros
Del ciego alado loco

Dulce como el recuerdo
Dulce como el olvido
Azul como el recuerdo
Azul como olvidar

Y mira

A Federico Hölderlin

To Friedrich Hölderlin

As distant from yourself
And as close
To that harsh sacred kingdom
Waiting for the sun
Next to an orange sky

So close

Waiting for the sun
Behind the wooden
Slats of a fence
Weeds on the ground

And you falter before it all
Before the sky
Before the two faces
Of the winged blind madman

Sweet as memory
Sweet as oblivion
Blue as memory
Blue as forgetting

And behold

Friedrich Hölderlin

Al fondo del valle
Brillando bajo el agua
Y los infinitos resplandores
Ciego como una estrella

Deep in the valley
Resplendent under the waters
And the infinite shimmering lights
Blind like a star

Anuncio

Gran Jefe Un Lado del Cielo
Interpretará *Trois*
Gymnopedies de Erik

Satie en un piano

Viejo y apolillado

La tribu Sioux invita
A Usted a oír
El manantial

Announcement

Big Chief One Side of The Sky
Will perform *Trois*
Gymnopedies by Erik

Satie on an ancient

Worm-eaten piano

The Sioux tribe invites
You to hear
The bubbling spring

Ars poética

Farbe, du wechselnde, Komm
Freundlich zum Menschen herab
SCHILLER

color, tú que cambias, ven
Amigable a los hombres

I

La Poesía es un Arte
Continuo: por ello plagio:

Consérvame en la solitud
De las costas abruptas
Y grises y de los mares

Sin sol, más aún,
Creo en el plagio

Y con el plagio creo,
Continúo, pleno
El aire de colores

Fromme gesunde Natur!

Y así he podido ver

[142]

Ars Poetica

Color, you who change, come
Amenable to all men

I

Poetry is a continuous
Art: that is why I plagiarize:

Hold me in the solitude
Of the rugged, grey
Coastlines and sunless

Seas, even more,
I believe in plagiarism

And with plagiarism I create,
I continue, the wind
Ablaze with colors

Fromme gesunde Natur!

And so I have seen

En cada mal suceso
Una esperanza

To know even hate
Is but a mask of Love

2

Cantas:
Y ese es tu brillo:

Así las flores
Suavemente

Habitan el jardín
Que hay en tus ojos
Y through your eyes
To your heart.

In every misfortune
A glimmer of hope

To know even hate
Is but a mask of Love

2

You sing out:
And that is when you shine:

Just as flowers
Gently

Inhabit the garden
Nestled in your eyes
And through your eyes
To your heart

Landscapes

1 *Lago de Constanza*

En Radolfzell am Bodensee
Entre las maderas
Brilla el agua

Y el cielo flamígero
Azul

Llega la luna
La luna oscura
Y roja

Y el agua desciende
Del cielo

Es la lluvia.

2 *Tübingen*

 a Hölderlin le fou

Desde la torre
Puede verse
El plumaje blanco

Landscapes

1 *Lake Constance*

In Radolfzell am Bodensee
Between slats of wood
The waters shimmer

And the flaming blue
Sky

The moon rises
The dark red
Moon

And water descends
From the heavens

It is rain.

2 *Tübingen*

       To Hölderlin le fou

From the tower
You can see
The white plumage

De los cisnes

Desde la taberna
Alguien contempla
Como una vez

Los cisnes

3 *Suiza*
 St. Maurice

A mi hermano Max

Entre los Alpes
La noche es más clara

Y hay una profundidad
De flores absinto
Violetas de genciana
Menta

El aire obscuro
De la noche

Es así con la dulzura
De la luna

Of the swans

From the tavern
Someone watches
As though for the first time

The swans

3 *Switzerland*
St. Maurice

To my brother Max

In the Alps
Night is clearer

And there is a depth
Of flowers absinthe
Gentian violets
Mint

Only the sweetness
Of the moon can make

The dark air of night
Like this

4 *Italia*
Bérgamo

Claro de luna
De Bérgamo

Espléndida

4 *Italy*
Bergamo

Claire de lune
Over Bergamo

Splendid

[Qué es aquella flor]

Qué es aquella flor
Que llevas
Pueda ser una flor
De lejanos días

Y te hablará de mí

Y tal vez te dijera

Shelley Álvarez estaba sentimental. Tal raro estado le
sobrevenía tan solo algunas veces. Quizás fuera verdad lo
que dice el valse:

Los afectos son leyes que gobiernan y mandan.

Porque cuando Shelley estaba sentimental llegaba aun a
aquel demoledor llamado recuerdo.

Qué es aquella flor que llevas
Pueda ser una flor,
Ya marchita de lejanos días

[What's that Flower]

What's that flower
You have on
Could it be a faded rose
From days gone by

And it shall speak to you of me

And perhaps it will say

Shelley Álvarez was feeling sentimental. This strange state
only rarely overcame him. Perhaps what the waltz says is
true:

Affect is a law that governs and rules.

Because when Shelley was feeling sentimental he would
always wind up in that devastating feeling called memory.

What's that flower
You have on
Could it be a faded rose

Y el afecto lo perturbaba estilísticamente. Una tarde, debido al sentimiento, olvidó un bemol y recordó alguna tristeza: pero el Preludio ganó algo: así debió soñarlo Federico Chopin en Palma de Mallorca: Qué es aquella flor que llevas.

From days gone by

And affect disturbed him stylistically. One afternoon, moved
by these feelings, he left off a B-flat notation and recalled a
certain sorrow: but the Prelude gained something: that must
be how Frederic Chopin dreamt it in Palma de Mallorca:
What's that flower you have on.

Stabat Máter

Stabat Máter
Esperando en la comisaría
Ante la sorna del alférez

Stabat Máter
Aguardando que concluya
La voraz semiología
De los médicos

Stabat Máter
Descuajeringada entregada
A obstetrices somnolientas

Stabat Máter
Sola en la noche

Stabat Máter
En las vitrinas
En el día de la madre

Stabat Máter
Once veces dolorosa

Stabat
Máter

Stabat Mater

Stabat Mater
Waiting in the police station
Under the sergeant's scornful eye

Stabat Mater
Awaiting the conclusion
Of the doctors'
Voracious semiology

Stabat Mater
Splayed ragged on the sleepy
Obstetricians' bench

Stabat Mater
Alone in the night

Stabat Mater
In shop windows
On Mothers' Day

Stabat Mater
Eleven times sorrowful

Stabat
Mater

7

A un suicida en una piscina

No mueras más
Oye una sinfonía para banda
Volverás a amarte cuando escuches
Diez trombones
Con su añil claridad
Entre la noche
Entreteje con su añil claridad
No mueras
Por lo que Dios más ame
Sal de las aguas
Sécate
Contémplate en el espejo
En el cual te ahogabas
Quédate en el tercer planeta
Tan sólo conocido
Por tener unos seres bellísimos
Que emiten sonidos con el cuello
Esa unión entre el cuerpo

VII

A un suicida en una piscina

No mueras más
Oye una sinfonía para banda
Volverás a amarte cuando escuches
Diez trombones
Con su añil claridad
Entre la noche
No mueras
Entreteje con su añil claridad
No mueras
Por lo que Dios más ame
Sal de las aguas
Sécate
Contémplate en el espejo
En el cual te ahogabas
Quédate en el tercer planeta
Tan sólo conocido
Por tener unos seres bellísimos
Que emiten sonidos con el cuello
Esa unión entre el cuerpo
Y los ensueños
Y con sus máquinas ingenuas
Que se llevan a los labios
O acarician con las manos
Arte purísimo

To a Suicide in a Swimming Pool

Die no more
Listen to a symphony for marching band
You will love yourself once more when you hear
Ten trombones
With their indigo clarity
In the night
Do not die
Weave into its indigo clarity
Do not die
In the name of what God loves best
Emerge from the waters
Towel off
Look into the mirror
Where you were drowning
Stay on the third planet
Known only
For its gorgeous beings
Who emit sounds from their throats
That hinge between body
And dreams
And with the innocent devices
They raise to their lips
Or stroke with their hands
Purest art

Llamado Música
No mueras más
Con su añil claridad

[Brian, 1971]

Called Music
Die no more
With its indigo clarity

[Brian, 1971]

* finis opus
laus deo

* autógrafo del autor

Luis hernandez

Note

Citing sources for *The School of Solitude: Collected Poems*

PUCP = Pontificia Universidad Católica del Perú digital archive of notebooks in facsimile reproduction;

VH = Luis Hernández, *Vox horrísona*, 3rd ed. Lima: Editorial Ave Fénix, 2007 (collected poetry)

1. Los Cowboys / Cowboys PUCP/VH
2. [Soy Luisito Hernández] / [This is Luisito Hernández] PUCP
3. [Y tú callabas] / [And you fell silent] PUCP
4. La canción / The Song PUCP/VH
5. Alambres / Wires PUCP
6. Apollon Musagète / Apollon Musagète PUCP/VH

Swan Isle Press is an independent, not-for-profit,
literary publisher dedicated to publishing works of poetry,
fiction and nonfiction that inspire and educate while
advancing the knowledge and appreciation of literature,
art, and culture. The Press's bilingual editions and single-
language English translations make contemporary and
classic texts more accessible to a variety of readers.

For more information on books of related interest
or for a catalog of new publications contact:

www.swanislepress.com

THE SCHOOL OF SOLITUDE

S   W   A   N
I   S   L   E
P   R   E   S   S

Designed by Andrea Guinn

Typeset in Dante

Printed on 55# Glatfelter Natural